Christmas
IN CROSS STITCH

Julie Hasler

MEREHURST

THE CHARTS
Some of the designs in this book are very detailed and due to
inevitable space limitations, the charts may be shown on a
comparatively small scale; in such cases, readers may find it
helpful to have the particular chart with which they are
currently working enlarged.

THREADS
The projects in this book were all stitched with DMC stranded cotton
embroidery threads. The keys given with each chart also list thread
combinations for those who wish to use Anchor or Madeira threads.
It should be pointed out that the shades produced by different
companies vary slightly, and it is not always possible to find
identical colours in a different range.

Published in 1994 by Merehurst Limited
Ferry House, 51-57 Lacy Road, Putney, London SW15 1PR
Text © Copyright 1994 Julie Hasler
Photography & illustrations © Copyright 1994 Merehurst Limited
ISBN 1 85391 372 3

A catalogue record for this book is available from the British Library.

Managing Editor Heather Dewhurst
Edited by Diana Lodge
Designed by Maggie Aldred
Photography by Marie-Louise Avery
Illustrations by John Hutchinson
Typesetting by Dacorum Type & Print, Hemel Hempstead
Colour separation by Fotographics Limited, UK – Hong Kong
Printed in Italy by G. Canale & C. S.p.A. - Borgaro T.se (Turin)

*Merehurst is the leading publisher of craft books and has an excellent range
of titles to suit all levels. Please send to the address above for our
free catalogue, stating the title of this book.*

CONTENTS

INTRODUCTION

Christmas is one of the happiest times of the year, for adults and, even more, for children. The church is lit with candles for the service which we call the Christ Mass; carol singers go from house to house, and people kiss under the mistletoe as traditional signs of friendship. We decorate our houses with holly wreaths and paper chains, and festoon the Christmas tree with glittering ornaments, tinsel and lights. We have a traditional Christmas dinner with all the family and friends gathered round, pull crackers, dress up in paper hats and afterwards, play games.

The most exciting part of all, for the children, is the giving and receiving of presents, just as the shepherds and kings gave presents to the new-born baby Jesus in Bethlehem nearly two thousand years ago. In celebration of the festive season, I have designed a whole range of Christmas projects, both for the home and to give as gifts.

Each cross stitch design is carefully charted and has an accompanying colour key and full instructions for making up the project. Also included is a Basic Skills section, which covers everything from how to prepare your fabric and stretch it in an embroidery hoop or frame, to mounting your cross stitch embroidery over card ready for display. Some of the designs are very simple and are aimed at beginners, others are more challenging, with many colours and shaded effects for the more experienced stitcher, or one who is eager to expand existing skills.

Whatever your level of skill or interest in the craft, you will enjoy being able to create items from the wide range of projects offered, suitable for children and adults of all ages.

BASIC SKILLS

BEFORE YOU BEGIN

PREPARING THE FABRIC
Even with an average amount of handling, many evenweave fabrics tend to fray at the edges, so it is a good idea to overcast the raw edges, using ordinary sewing thread, before you begin.

THE INSTRUCTIONS
Each project begins with a full list of the materials that you will require; Aida, Tula, Lugana and Linda are all fabrics produced by Zweigart. Note that the measurements given for the embroidery fabric include a minimum of 3cm (1¼in) all around to allow for stretching it in a frame and preparing the edges to prevent them from fraying.

Colour keys for stranded embroidery cottons – DMC, Anchor or Madeira – are given with each chart. It is assumed that you will need to buy one skein of each colour mentioned, even though you may use less, but where two or more skeins are needed, this information is included in the main list of requirements.

To work from the charts, particularly those where several symbols are used in close proximity, some readers may find it helpful to have the chart enlarged so that the squares and symbols can be seen more easily. Many photocopying services will do this for a minimum charge.

Before you begin to embroider, always mark the centre of the design with two lines of basting stitches, one vertical and one horizontal, running from edge to edge of the fabric, as indicated by the arrows on the charts.

As you stitch, use the centre lines given on the chart and the basting threads on your fabric as reference points for counting the squares and threads to position your design accurately.

WORKING IN A HOOP
A hoop is the most popular frame for use with small areas of embroidery. It consists of two rings, one fitted inside the other; the outer ring usually has an adjustable screw attachment so that it can be tightened to hold the stretched fabric in place. Hoops are available in several sizes, ranging from

10cm (4in) in diameter to quilting hoops with a diameter of 38cm (15in). Hoops with table stands or floor stands attached are also available.

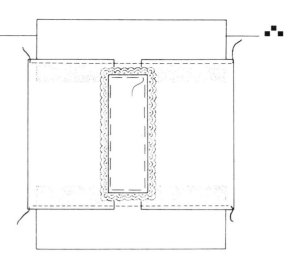

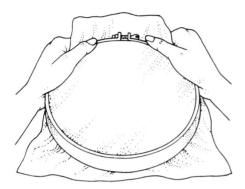

1 To stretch your fabric in a hoop, place the area to be embroidered over the inner ring and press the outer ring over it with the tension screw released. Tissue paper can be placed between the outer ring and the embroidery, so that the hoop does not mark the fabric. Lay the tissue paper over the fabric when you set it in the hoop, then tear away the central embroidery area.

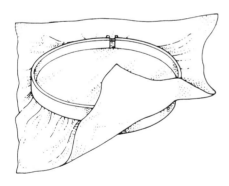

2 Smooth the fabric and, if needed, straighten the grain before tightening the screw. The fabric should be evenly stretched.

EXTENDING EMBROIDERY FABRIC
It is easy to extend a piece of embroidery fabric, such as a bookmark, to stretch it in a hoop.

● Fabric oddments of a similar weight can be used. Simply cut four pieces to size (in other words, to the measurement that will fit both the embroidery fabric and your hoop) and baste them to each side of the embroidery fabric before stretching it in the hoop in the usual way.

WORKING IN A RECTANGULAR FRAME
Rectangular frames are more suitable for larger pieces of embroidery. They consist of two rollers, with tapes attached, and two flat side pieces, which slot into the rollers and are held in place by pegs or screw attachments. Available in different sizes, either alone or with adjustable table or floor stands, frames are measured by the length of the roller tape, and range in size from 30cm (12in) to 68cm (27in).

As alternatives to a slate frame, canvas stretchers and the backs of old picture frames can be used. Provided there is sufficient extra fabric around the finished size of the embroidery, the edges can be turned under and simply attached with drawing pins (thumb tacks) or staples.

1 To stretch your fabric in a rectangular frame, cut out the fabric, allowing at least an extra 5cm (2in) all around the finished size of the embroidery. Baste a single 12mm (½in) turning on the top and bottom edges and oversew strong tape, 2.5cm (1in) wide, to the other two sides. Mark the centre line both ways with basting stitches. Working from the centre outwards and using strong thread, oversew the top and bottom edges to the roller tapes. Fit the side pieces into the slots, and roll any extra fabric on one roller until the fabric is taut.

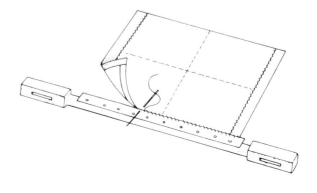

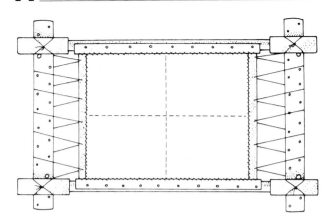

2 Insert the pegs or adjust the screw attachments to secure the frame. Thread a large-eyed needle (chenille needle) with strong thread or fine string and lace both edges, securing the ends around the intersections of the frame. Lace the webbing at 2.5cm (1in) intervals, stretching the fabric evenly.

ENLARGING A GRAPH PATTERN

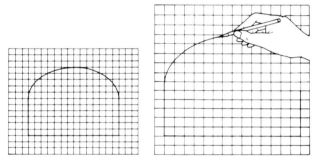

● To enlarge a graph pattern, you will need a sheet of graph paper ruled in 1cm (⅜in) squares, a ruler and pencil. If, for example, the scale is one square to 5cm (2in) you should first mark the appropriate lines to give a grid of the correct size. Copy the graph freehand from the small grid to the larger one, completing one square at a time. Use a ruler to draw the straight lines first, and then copy the freehand curves.

TO BIND AN EDGE

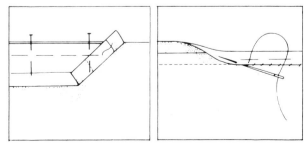

1 Open out the turning on one edge of the bias binding and pin in position on the right side of the fabric, matching the fold to the seamline. Fold over the cut end of the binding. Finish by overlapping the starting point by about 12mm (½in). Baste and machine stitch along the seamline.

2 Fold the binding over the raw edge to the wrong side, baste and, using matching sewing thread, neatly hem to finish.

PIPED SEAMS
Contrasting piping adds a special decorative finish to a seam and looks particularly attractive on items such as cushions and cosies.

You can cover piping cord with either bias-cut fabric of your choice or a bias binding; alternatively, ready-covered piping cord is available in several widths and many colours.

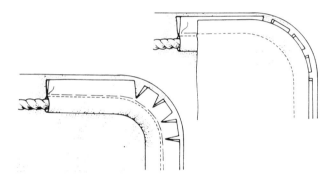

1 To apply piping, pin and baste it to the right side of the fabric, with seam lines matching. Clip into the seam allowance where necessary.

2 With right sides together, place the second piece of fabric on top, enclosing the piping. Baste and then either hand stitch in place or machine stitch, using a zipper foot. Stitch as close to the piping as possible, covering the first line of stitching.

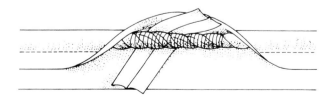

3 To join ends of piping cord together, first overlap the two ends by about 2.5cm (1in). Unpick the two cut ends of bias to reveal the cord. Join the bias strip as shown. Trim and press the seam open. Unravel and splice the two ends of the cord. Fold the bias strip over it, and finish basting around the edge.

MOUNTING EMBROIDERY

The cardboard should be cut to the size of the finished embroidery, with an extra 6mm (¼in) added all around to allow for the recess in the frame.

LIGHTWEIGHT FABRICS

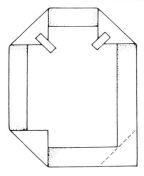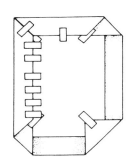

1 Place the emboidery face down, with the cardboard centred on top, and basting and pencil lines matching. Begin by folding over the fabric at each corner and securing it with masking tape.

2 Working first on one side and then the other, fold over the fabric on all sides and secure it firmly with pieces of masking tape, placed about 2.5cm (1in) apart. Also neaten the mitred corners with masking tape, pulling the fabric tightly to give a firm, smooth finish.

HEAVIER FABRICS

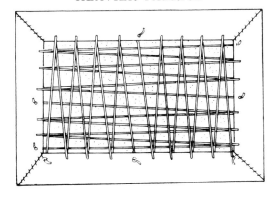

● Lay the embroidery face down, with the cardboard centred on top; fold over the edges of the fabric on opposite sides, making mitred folds at the corners, and lace across, using strong thread. Repeat on the other two sides. Finally, pull up the stitches fairly tightly to stretch the fabric firmly over the cardboard. Overstitch the mitred corners.

CROSS STITCH

For all cross stitch embroidery, the following two methods of working are used. In each case, neat rows of vertical stitches are produced on the back of the fabric.

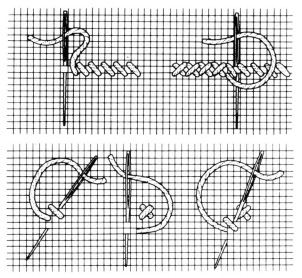

● When stitching large areas, work in horizontal rows. Working from right to left, complete the first row of evenly spaced diagonal stitches over the number of threads specified in the project instructions. Then, working from left to right, repeat the process. Continue in this way, making sure each stitch crosses in the same direction.

● When stitching diagonal lines, work downwards, completing each stitch before moving to the next.

BACKSTITCH

Backstitch is used in the projects to give emphasis to a particular foldline, an outline or a shadow. The stitches are worked over the same number of threads as the cross stitch, forming continuous straight or diagonal lines.

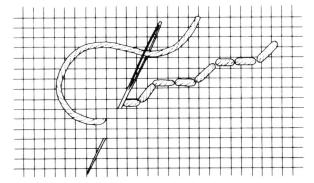

● Make the first stitch from left to right; pass the needle behind the fabric, and bring it out one stitch length ahead to the left. Repeat and continue in this way along the line.

Festive Table Linen

A set of hand-embroidered Christmas table linen, complete in every detail – even individual placecards – will delight your family and guests, and set the scene for one of the happiest days of the year.

FESTIVE TABLE LINEN

YOU WILL NEED

For the set of six plastic napkin holders, placecards and placemats, and the single table runner (sizes given below):

Six napkin holders
15cm × 7cm (6in × 3in) of white, 22-count Hardanger fabric (sufficient for six napkin holders)
15cm × 7cm (6in × 3in) of ultra-soft, medium-weight, iron-on interfacing, to back the napkin holders
Six red placecards, with 2.3cm (⅞in) circular cut-outs
15cm × 10cm (6in × 4in) of white, 18-count Aida fabric (sufficient for six placecards)
15cm × 10cm (6in × 4in) of ultra-soft, medium-weight, iron-on interfacing, to back the placecards
Six 40.6cm (16in) square dinner napkins
Six 33cm × 48.5cm (13in × 19in) placemats
33cm × 96.5cm (13in × 38in) table runner
Stranded embroidery cotton in the colours given in the panel
No 26 tapestry needle

NOTE The napkin holders, placecards, napkins, placemats and runner are all obtainable from specialist suppliers, see page 48.

●

NAPKIN HOLDERS

Using rows of basting stitches, divide the Hardanger fabric into six equal sections. Take the holly design from the Christmas bows border, and embroider one holly motif at the centre of each section, using two strands of embroidery cotton in the needle throughout.

Press the finished embroidery. Iron the interfacing to the back of the fabric, then cut along the basted lines to separate the six holders. For each holder, trim the fabric to measure 4.3cm × 3.8cm (1⅝in × 1½in), and place the embroidery inside the clear plastic holder.

PLACECARDS

Using rows of basting stitches, divide the Aida fabric into six equal sections. Take the holly design from the Christmas bows border, and embroider one motif at the centre of each section,

using two strands of embroidery cotton in the needle throughout.

Press the finished embroidery. Iron the interfacing to the back of the fabric, then cut along the basted lines to separate the six holders. For each placecard, trim the fabric to measure 4cm (1½in) square.

Position your design behind the round aperture. When you are happy that it is correctly centred, use a small piece of clear tape to hold it while you seal the card. Remove the backing strip from the panel on the left of the placecard; fold it over, and press firmly to seal the two halves of the placecard together. You can then add the names or wording you require, perhaps using a gold or silver pen.

TABLE LINEN

All of the designs are stitched over two threads of the 26-count fabric used for these ready-prepared table linens, and two strands of embroidery cotton are used in the needle throughout.

The dinner napkins feature the Christmas bows border, which runs along the side edges, 2.5cm (1in) in from the fringe.

For the placemats, embroider the holly border, again placing it along the side edges, 2.5cm (1in) in from the fringe.

For the table runner, start by marking the centre with two lines of basting stitches (see page 4). Stitch the holly wreath at the centre of the runner, then measure out for 25.5cm (10in) on each side of the central vertical line. Stitch the holly border at this point on each side of the runner.

When you have completed the holly borders, embroider a Christmas bows border down each side, 2.5cm (1in) out from the holly border, and the same distance in from the fringed edge.

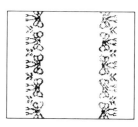

Napkin

Placemat

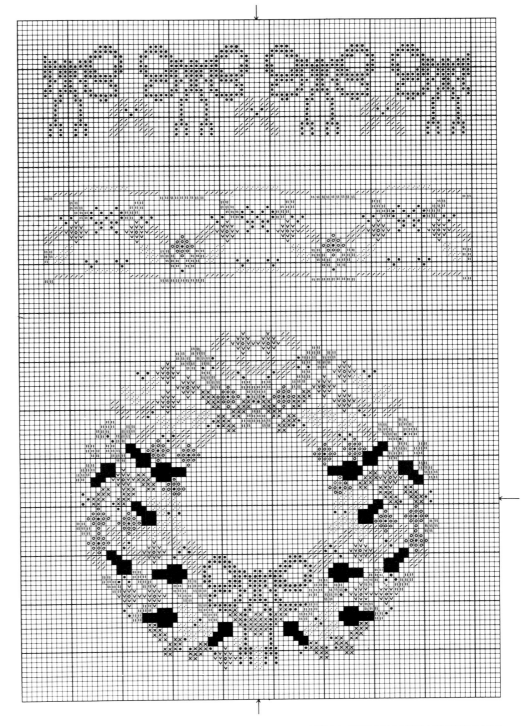

Table Runner

TABLE LINEN ▲		DMC	ANCHOR	MADEIRA
●	Bright orange red	606	335	0209
.•	Bright Christmas green	704	256	1308
╱	Kelly green	702	226	1306
‖	Christmas green	699	923	1303
☑	Bright canary yellow	973	297	0105
◯	Medium tangerine orange	941	304	0203
☒	Light loden green	3364	843	1603
■	Khaki	370	888	2112

11

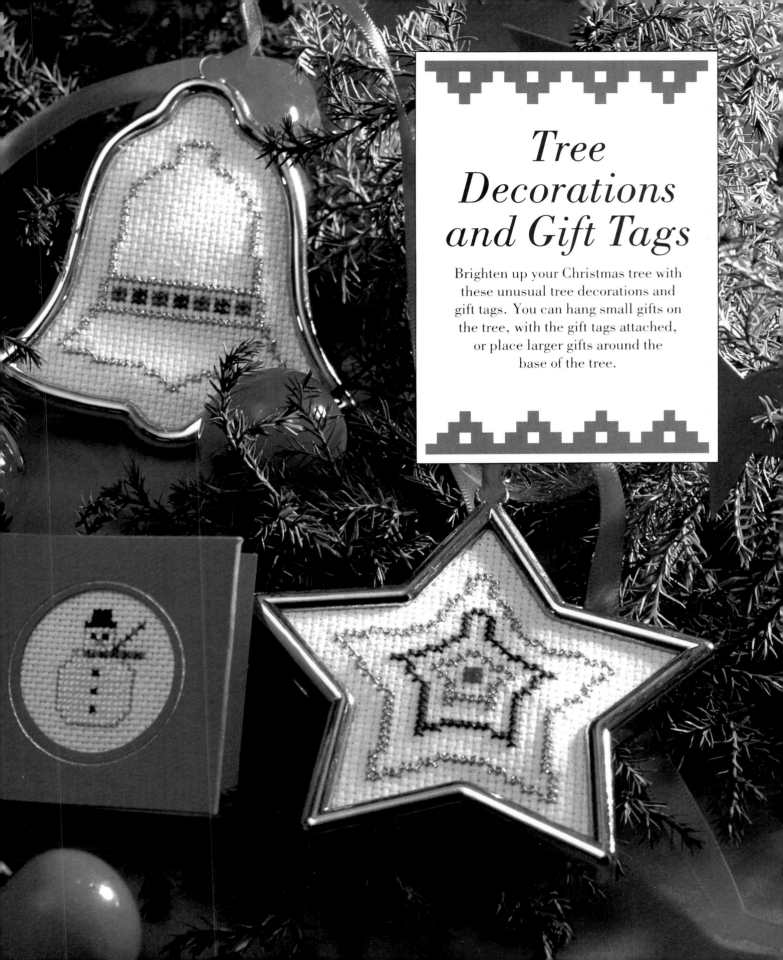

Tree Decorations and Gift Tags

Brighten up your Christmas tree with these unusual tree decorations and gift tags. You can hang small gifts on the tree, with the gift tags attached, or place larger gifts around the base of the tree.

TREE DECORATIONS AND GIFT TAGS

YOU WILL NEED

For three tree decorations, each measuring approximately 9cm × 8cm (3½in × 3¼in):

38cm × 13cm (15in × 5in) of white, 16-count Aida fabric
38cm × 13cm (15in × 5in) of medium-weight iron-on fabric interfacing
60cm (24in) of red ribbon, 6mm (¼in) wide
Stranded embroidery cotton in the colours given in the appropriate panels
Gold metallic thread
No 26 tapestry needle
Framecraft 'Christmas shapes' – tree, Santa and bell (for suppliers, see page 48)

For four gift tags, each measuring 5cm (2in), with an aperture measuring 4½cm (1¼in):

13cm (5in) square of white Hardanger fabric, with 22 threads to 2.5cm (1in)
13cm (5in) square of medium-weight iron-on fabric interfacing
Stranded embroidery cotton in the colours given in the appropriate panels
Gold metallic thread
No 26 tapestry needle

TREE DECORATIONS

Divide the Aida strip into three square sections, using lines of basting stitches. With two strands of embroidery cotton in the needle, complete the cross stitch embroidery, making sure that each design is centred within its section. Iron the interfacing to the wrong side of the fabric, to prevent it from fraying, and then cut along the basted lines to separate the three designs.

Place each Christmas shape over the relevant embroidered design, ensuring that the embroidered design is centred within the shape, and draw around the edge of the shape with a soft pencil.

For each shape, take the paper template provided; centre this within your pencil lines, and draw around this with a soft pencil. This is your cutting line. Cut your fabric to size carefully and place it, right side down, into the shape. Place the paper template on to the reverse side of your embroidery. Next, peel the backing off the felt, and carefully place it over the back of the 'Christmas shape'. Thread the ribbon through the hole, ready for hanging the shape on the tree.

TREE DECORATIONS ▼	DMC	ANCHOR	MADEIRA
● Gold thread	—	—	—
⊞ Bright Christmas green	700	229	1304
☒ Bright Christmas red	666	46	0210
∴ Silver thread	—	—	—
☑ Dark violet	552	100	0713

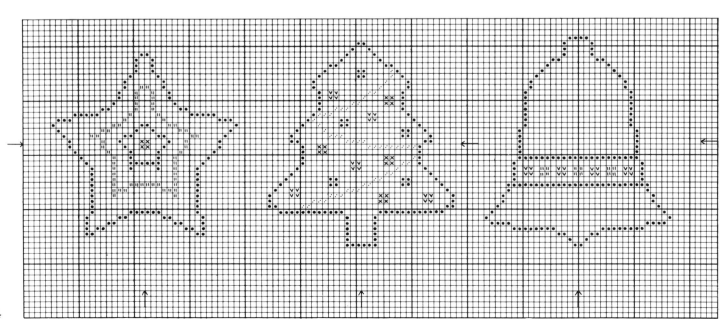

NÖEL ▶		DMC	ANCHOR	MADEIRA
⊿	Dark Kelly green	701	227	1305
⊽	Bright Christmas red	666	46	0210

Note: bks lettering in bright Christmas red.

SNOWMAN ▶		DMC	ANCHOR	MADEIRA
⊙	Black	310	403	Black
⊽	Pumpkin orange	971	316	0203
⊿	Bright Christmas red	666	46	0210
∥	Dark Kelly green	701	227	1305
⋮	White	White	2	White
	Light steel grey*	318	399	1802

Note: bks with light steel grey (used for bks only).*

GIFT TAGS

Divide your Hardanger into four equal sections, using horizontal and vertical lines of basting stitches. Complete the cross stitch embroidery, with one strand of embroidery cotton in the needle throughout, ensuring that each design is centred within a section. Press your finished embroidery, and then iron the interfacing to the wrong side of your fabric, to prevent it from fraying. Cut along the basted lines to separate the four designs.

For each design, place the embroidery so that it shows through the aperture in the gift tag. Use a soft pencil to mark cutting lines on the wrong side of the fabric, slightly larger than the aperture, and then trim to size. Place the design in position again. It helps if you use a small piece of clear adhesive tape to hold part of your design in position before you seal the two halves together. Remove the backing strip from the panel on the left; fold it over, and press firmly to seal the two halves of the gift tag together. You can add a piece of embroidery silk or narrow ribbon to complete the gift tag.

PUDDING ▶		DMC	ANCHOR	MADEIRA
∥	Dark Kelly green	701	227	1305
C	Bright Christmas red	666	46	0210
⋮	White	White	2	White
	Light steel grey*	318	399	1802
⊿	Medium brown	433	371	2008
⊙	Dark forest brown	938	381	2005

Note: bks with light steel grey (used for bks only).*

REINDEER ▶		DMC	ANCHOR	MADEIRA
⋮	White	White	2	White
	Light steel grey*	318	399	1802
⊙	Black	310	403	Black
⊽	Bright Christmas red	666	46	0210
⊿	Beige brown	840	379	1912
∥	Spice brown	3064	914	2312

Note: bks with light steel grey (used for bks only).*

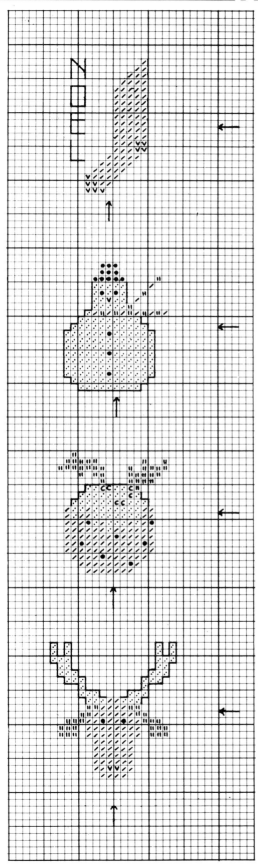

15

Glass Jars and Decorative Mats

These beautiful cut-glass lead crystal jars, accompanied by pretty mats, make gifts which are both useful and decorative. They can adorn a dressing table, an occasional table or even a mantelpiece. Why not fill them with brightly coloured sweets for a child?

GLASS JARS AND DECORATIVE MATS

YOU WILL NEED

For each cut-glass jar, with a lid measuring 6.5cm (2⅝in) in diameter:

10cm (4in) square of ecru, 25-count Lugana fabric
Stranded embroidery cotton in the colours given in the appropriate panel
No26 tapestry needle

For each mat, measuring 16cm (6¼in) square:

16cm (6¼in) square of Christmas red, 14-count Aida fabric
Stranded embroidery cotton in the colour given in the appropriate panel
No24 tapestry needle

•

GLASS JARS

For each design, prepare the fabric, marking the centre with basting stitches, and stretch it in a hoop (see page 4). Using one strand of embroidery cotton in the needle throughout, complete your chosen design. Press the finished embroidery, leaving the basting stitches in place.

ASSEMBLING THE LID

Gently remove all parts from the glass jar lid. Centre the design within the lid, and draw around the outer edge, marking the fabric. Remove the lid and cut the fabric to size. To assemble the lid, replace the clear acetate and place your design in the lid, with the right side against the acetate. Place the sponge behind your design. Push the metal locking disc very firmly into place, using thumb pressure, with the raised side of the disc facing the sponge. When the locking disc is tightly in position, use a little glue to secure the flock lid lining card.

DECORATIVE MATS

For each mat, complete the cross stitch embroidery, working from the centre outwards and using two strands of embroidery cotton. Press if required and then fray the edges by removing threads, one at a time, to a depth of 6mm (¼in). You can either leave the frayed edge as it is, or secure it with hemstitching, using a matching thread.

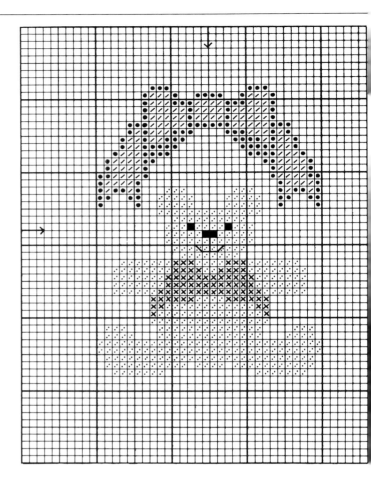

GLASS JARS ▲		DMC	ANCHOR	MADEIRA
■	Black	310	403	Black
●	Bright Christmas green	700	229	1304
╱	Chartreuse	703	238	1307
⠂	Christmas gold	783	307	2211
✕	Bright Christmas red	666	46	0210
‖	Steel grey	414	400	1801
C	Pale grey	415	398	1803

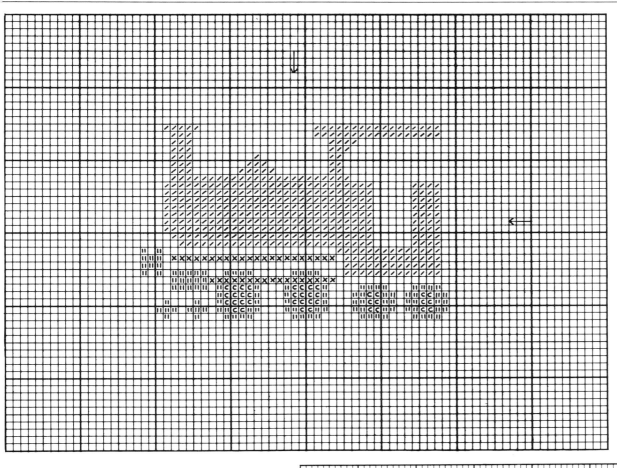

MAT ▶	DMC	ANCHOR	MADEIRA
■ White	White	2	White

19

Christmas Crackers

These pretty Christmas crackers
offer a novel way of wrapping gifts.
Each cracker can be filled with
sweets, jewellery or other small gifts.

CHRISTMAS CRACKERS

For each cracker, measuring 22.5cm (9in) long and 4cm (1⅝in) in diameter:

28cm × 19cm (11in × 7½in) of white, holly green or Christmas red, 14-count Aida fabric
112cm (44in) of red or green ribbon, 6mm (¼in) wide
Stranded embroidery cotton in the colours given in the appropriate panel
Gold metallic thread
No 24 tapestry needle
Cardboard tube from the centre of a toilet roll
Double-sided tape

●

THE EMBROIDERY

Prepare the fabric, marking the centre with basting stitches, and stretch it in a hoop (see page 4). Using two strands of embroidery cotton in the needle throughout, complete your chosen design. Remove basting stitches and press the finished embroidery, pressing a 12mm (½in) seam allowance to the wrong side down each long edge.

MAKING THE CRACKER

Fray the two short edges for 2.5cm (1in), removing the cross threads of the Aida one at a time.

Place the embroidery face down on a firm, flat surface. Put a strip of double-sided tape along the complete length of one of the pressed seam allowances (on the wrong side of the embroidery).

Put another strip of double-sided tape along the length of the cardboard tube. Lay the taped tube against the seam allowance. Make sure that the tube is centred, so that an equal amount of fabric extends beyond the tube at each end.

Carefully roll the fabric around the tube, pressing the taped seam allowance firmly where the fabric meets.

Cut the ribbon into two equal lengths; take one length and tie it in a bow around one end of the cracker. Place your gift inside the cardboard tube, and tie the remaining length of ribbon into a bow around the other end of the cracker, which is now ready to be hung on the tree.

ROBIN ▶		DMC	ANCHOR	MADEIRA
‖	Very light topaz yellow	727	293	0110
⁄	Light emerald green	912	209	1212
●	Light red	350	11	0213
■	Black	310	403	Black
⦂	Medium cocoa brown	407	882	2310
C	Chocolate	632	936	2311
◤	Dark beige brown	839	905	1913

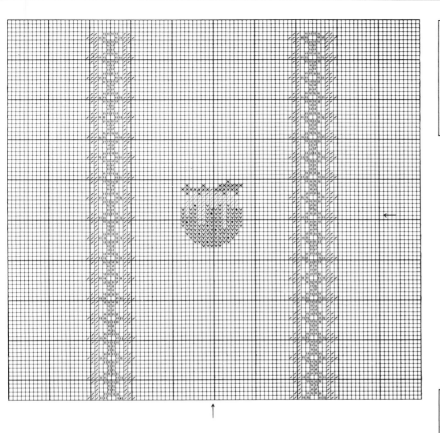

PUDDING ◀		DMC	ANCHOR	MADEIRA
╱	Red	349	13	0212
‖	Gold thread	—	—	—
☒	Light chartreuse			
	green	704	256	1308
⊡	White	White	2	White
∨	Tan brown	436	363	2011
●	Dark coffee brown	801	357	2007

WREATH ▼		DMC	ANCHOR	MADEIRA
╲	Chartreuse	703	238	1307
☒	Red	349	13	0212
⊡	White	White	2	White

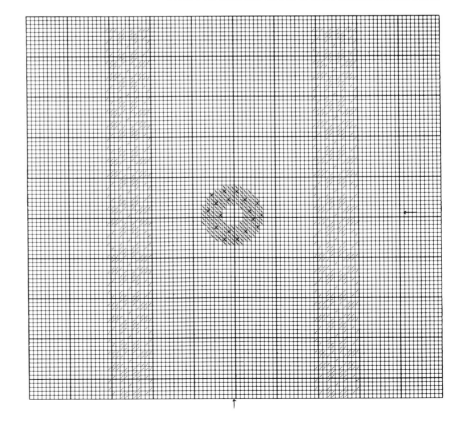

Quilted Wall Hanging

In days gone by, Christmas used to go on for twelve days and nights, until January. The song 'The First Day of Christmas' highlights this traditional time, the new line of each verse telling of an amazing gift that the lady was sent on each day.

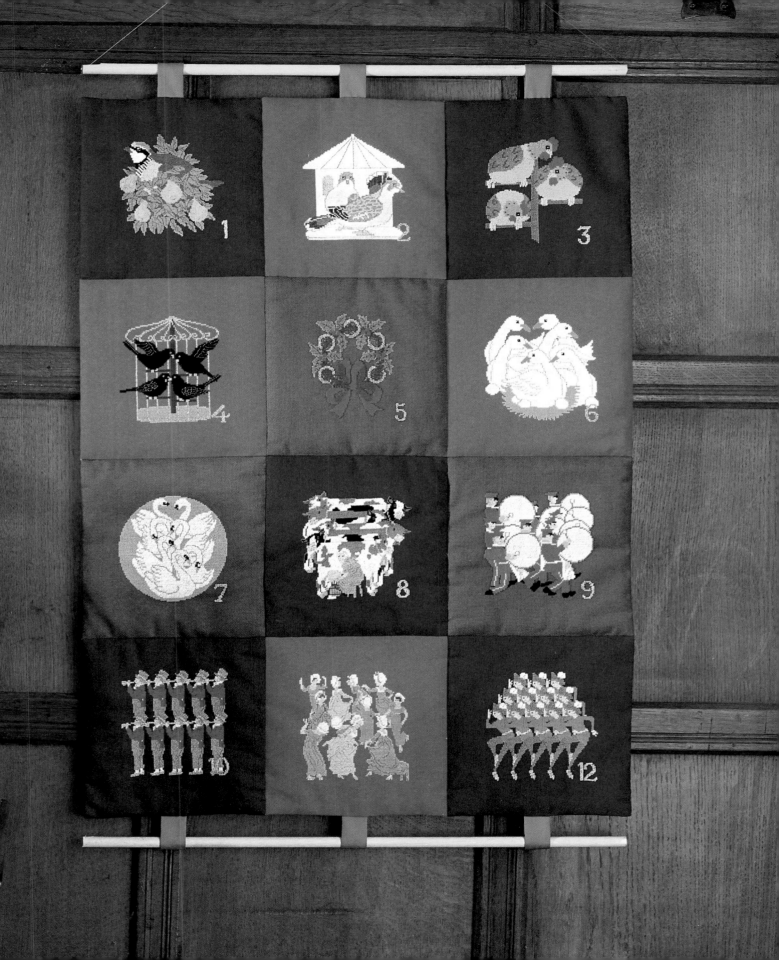

QUILTED WALL HANGING

YOU WILL NEED

For the wall hanging, measuring 61cm × 81.5cm (24in × 32in):

23cm (9in) squares of 18-count Aida fabric – five of navy, four of Christmas red, and three of holly green
71cm × 84cm (28in × 33in) of green cotton fabric, for the backing and hanging loops
63.5cm × 84cm (25in × 33in) of thin batting
Stranded embroidery cotton in the colours given in the appropriate panel
Gold and silver metallic threads
No26 tapestry needle
Two 60cm (23⅝in) lengths of dowling
White quilting thread

•

THE EMBROIDERY

One by one, prepare each Aida square, marking the centre with horizontal and vertical lines of basting stitches, and set it in a hoop or frame (see page 4). Embroider one of the designs on the square, using two strands of embroidery cotton in the needle for cross stitch, and finishing with the backstitching, made with one strand only in the needle. When you have embroidered all the squares, press each finished embroidery gently on the wrong side, using a steam iron.

MAKING THE HANGING

Position the designs as shown in the photograph. Join the squares in horizontal rows, taking 12mm (½in) seam allowances and pressing all seams to one side, then join the horizontal rows. For hanging loops, cut six strips of green cotton, each 7.7cm × 11.5cm (3in × 4½in). Also from green fabric, cut a piece measuring 63.5cm × 84cm (25in × 33in) for the backing. Fold each green strip in half lengthwise, right sides facing, and stitch down the long side. Turn right side out and press.

Lay the backing right side down on a flat surface. Smooth it out; place the batting on top, and then the embroidery, right side up. Pin the three layers together, and baste diagonally across from corner to corner, and straight across from edge to edge, and then in rectangles, starting close to the centre and spaced about 10cm (4in) apart. Using the quilting thread, quilt by hand or machine along the lines joining the squares, stopping 2.5cm (1in) away from the outer edge of the quilt.

Trim the batting to measure 63.5 × 84cm (24in × 32in). Bring the edge of the backing over the batting. Fold the hanging strips so that the short edges meet and position three at the top and three at the bottom of the hanging, concealing the raw edges between the batting/backing and the top fabric. Stitch the loops firmly to the batting/backing layers. Fold in the raw edge of the top fabric all around, and slipstitch in place, making sure that the stitches do not show on the right side.

Place the lengths of dowling through the loops, to complete your wall hanging.

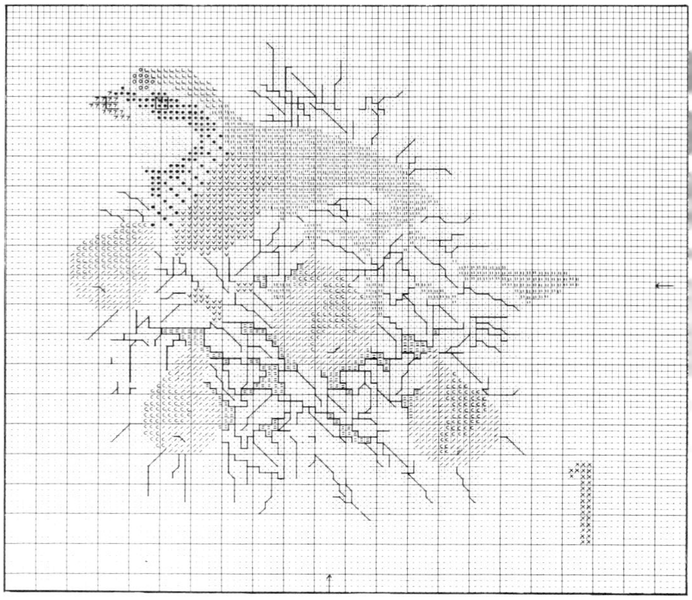

FIRST DAY OF CHRISTMAS ▲		DMC	ANCHOR	MADEIRA
‖	Avocado leaf brown	830	277	2114
☒	Gold thread	—	—	—
●	Black	310	403	Black
L	Light copper	922	324	0310
⁄	Golden brown	977	307	2301
	Dark golden brown*	975	352	2303
C	Topaz yellow	725	306	0108
•	Light forest green	989	256	1401
	Dark green*	319	246	1313
V	Light old gold	676	891	2208
☰	Dark forest green	987	245	1403
⁚	White	White	2	White
O	Pale grey	415	398	1803
7	Medium copper	920	339	0312
	Very dark beaver grey*	844	401	1810

Note: bks golden brown in dark golden brown; light forest green in dark green*, and medium copper in very dark beaver grey* (starred colours used for backstitching only).*

SECOND DAY OF CHRISTMAS ◄		DMC	ANCHOR	MADEIRA
⊿	Very light pearl grey	762	397	1804
•	White	White	2	White
☒	Gold thread	—	—	—
■	Black	310	403	Black
C	Pale blue	794	120	0907
V	Baby pink	818	48	0502
I	Light baby pink	819	892	0501
●	Very dark steel grey	413	401	1713
Z	Medium blue	826	161	1012
◣	Topaz yellow	725	306	0108
‖	Pale grey	415	398	1803
L	Light steel grey	318	399	1802
	Steel grey*	414	400	1801
≡	Dark forest brown	938	381	2005
⦂•	Light old gold	676	891	2208
O	Dark old gold	680	901	2210
N	Avocado leaf brown	830	277	2114
∧	Light salmon red	761	8	0404

Note: bks around eyes in black; other backstitching is in steel grey* (used for bks only).

THIRD DAY OF CHRISTMAS ►		DMC	ANCHOR	MADEIRA
☒	Gold thread	—	—	—
■	Black	310	403	Black
⊿	Topaz yellow	725	306	0108
•	White	White	2	White
●	Dark electric blue	995	410	1102
‖	Bright orange red	606	335	0209
⦂•	Dark hazelnut brown	420	375	2104
I	Light old gold	676	891	2208
	Medium topaz brown*	782	307	2212
V	Very dark copper	918	341	0314
C	Tangerine orange	740	316	0202
≡	Copper	921	338	0311

Note: bks in medium topaz brown* (used for bks only).

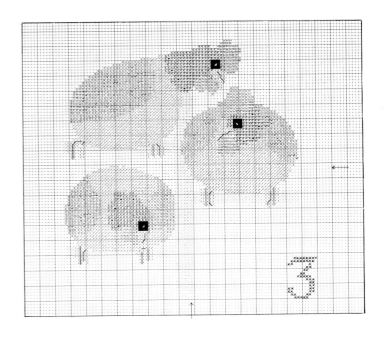

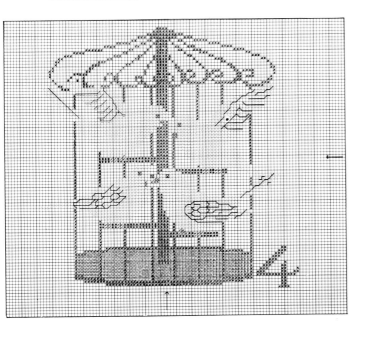

FOURTH DAY OF CHRISTMAS ◄		DMC	ANCHOR	MADEIRA
☒	Gold thread	—	—	—
●	Very dark coffee brown	898	360	2006
‖	Dark old gold	680	901	2210
C	Light old gold	676	891	2208
V	Very dark mahogany brown	300	352	2304
⊿	Pale grey	415	398	1803
	Steel grey*	414	400	1801
•	Black	310	403	Black

Note: bks with steel grey* (used for bks only).

The first day of Christmas,
my true love sent to me
A partridge in a pear tree

The second day of
Christmas, my true love
sent to me
Two turtle doves and a
partridge in a pear tree

The third day of Christmas,
my true love sent to me
Three French hens, two
turtle doves and a partridge
in a pear tree

The fourth day of
Christmas, my true love
sent to me
Four colly birds, three
French hens, etc.

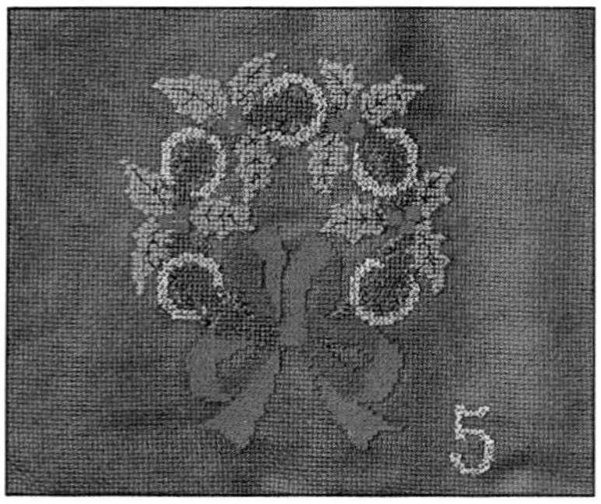

The fifth day of Christmas,
my true love sent to me
Five gold rings, four colly
birds, etc.

The sixth day of Christmas,
my true love sent to me
Six geese a-laying, five
gold rings, etc

FIFTH DAY OF CHRISTMAS ►	DMC	ANCHOR	MADEIRA
☒ Gold thread	—	—	—
◫ Medium garnet red	815	43	0513
Dark garnet red*	814	44	0514
Ⓒ Bright Christmas red	666	46	0210
⧄ Christmas green	699	923	1303
⊡ Kelly green	702	226	1306
Very dark evergreen*	890	218	1314
Green metallic Kreinik Balger Cord* 008C			

Note: backstitch leaf veins in very dark evergreen; around medium garnet red with dark garnet red*, and around all leaves with two strands of Kreinik green metallic* (starred colours used for bks only).*

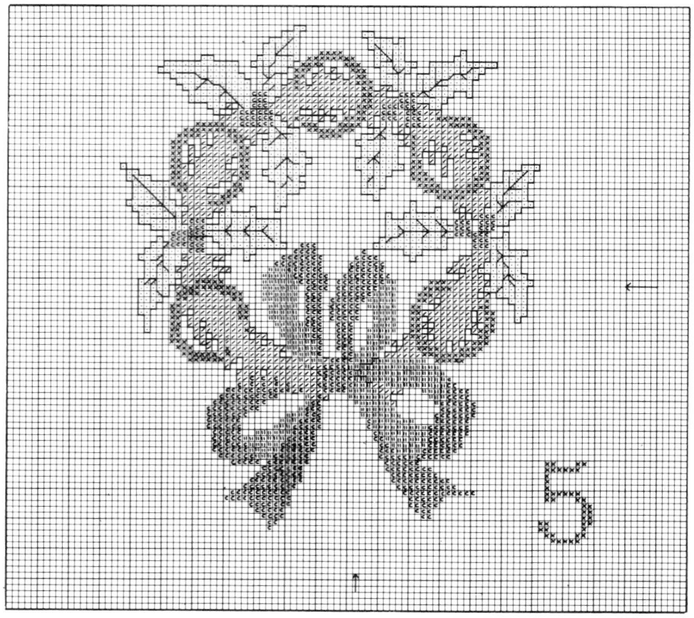

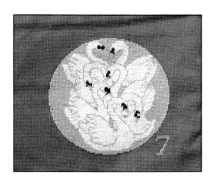

The seventh day of
Christmas, my true love
sent to me
Seven swans a-swimming,
six geese a-laying, etc

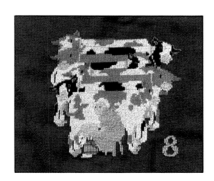

The eighth day of
Christmas, my true love
sent to me
Eight maids a-milking, seven
swans a-swimming, etc

The ninth day of
Christmas, my true love
sent to me
Nine drummers drumming,
eight maids a-milking, etc

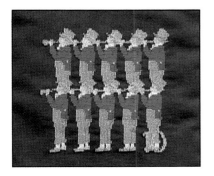

The tenth day of Christmas,
my true love sent to me
Ten pipers piping, nine
drummers drumming, etc

The eleventh day of
Christmas, my true love
sent to me
Eleven ladies dancing, ten
pipers piping, etc

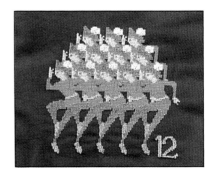

The twelfth day of
Christmas, my true love
sent to me
Twelve lords a-leaping,
eleven ladies dancing, ten
pipers piping, nine
drummers drumming, eight
maids a-milking, seven
swans a-swimming, six
geese a-laying, five gold
rings, four colly birds,
three French hens, two
turtle doves, and a
partridge in a pear tree.

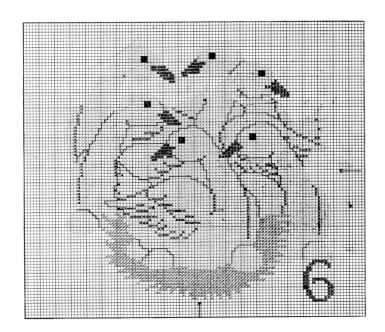

SIXTH DAY OF CHRISTMAS ◀		DMC	ANCHOR	MADEIRA
■	Black	310	403	Black
☒	Gold thread	—	—	—
•	White	White	2	White
	Medium steel grey*	317	400	1714
⊙	Pumpkin orange	971	316	0203
Ⅱ	Pale grey	415	398	1803
╱	Christmas gold	783	307	2211

Note: bks around white with steel grey* (used for bks only).

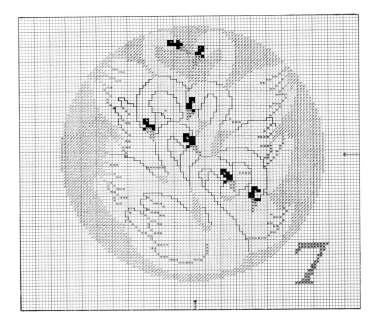

SEVENTH DAY OF CHRISTMAS ▶	DMC	ANCHOR	MADEIRA
☒ Gold thread	—	—	—
⧄ Aqua	959	186	1113
⧌ Medium tangerine orange	741	304	0201
■ Black	310	403	Black
⊡ White	White	2	White
Medium steel grey*	317	400	1714
‖ Pale grey	415	398	1803

Note: bks around white in medium steel grey (used for bks only).*

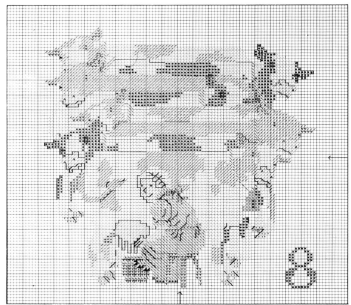

EIGHTH DAY OF CHRISTMAS ▶	DMC	ANCHOR	MADEIRA
☒ Gold thread	—	—	—
⧄ Medium golden brown	976	309	2302
Very dark copper*	918	341	0314
⊡ White	White	2	White
Light steel grey*	318	399	1802
⦂ Light peach	754	6	0305
Medium peach*	352	9	0303
⬤ Black	310	403	Black
⧌ Dark golden brown	975	352	2303
⧅ Delft blue	809	130	0909
Dark Delft blue*	798	146	0911
⊟ Christmas gold	783	307	2211
H Light topaz yellow	726	295	0109
‖ Pale grey	415	398	1803
OL Medium brown	433	371	2008
C Medium pink	899	27	0505
Very dark rose red*	326	59	0508
I Golden wheat	3046	887	2206
Dark golden wheat*	3045	888	2103
Y Tan brown	436	363	2011
◪ Very dark coffee brown	898	360	2006
Z Steel grey	414	400	1801

Note: bks around medium golden brown with very dark copper; around white and black with light steel grey*; around light peach with medium peach*; around Delft blue with very dark Delft blue*; around medium pink with very dark rose red*; around golden wheat with dark golden wheat*, and around tan brown with medium brown (starred colours used for bks only).*

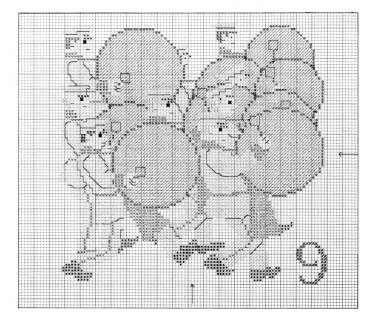

NINTH DAY OF CHRISTMAS ▶	DMC	ANCHOR	MADEIRA
☒ Gold thread	—	—	—
O Medium topaz brown	782	307	2212
Dark golden brown*	975	352	2303
⬤ Black	310	403	Black
Steel grey*	414	400	1801
⧄ Off white	746	368	0101
Golden wheat*	3046	887	2206
⦂ Bright orange red	606	335	0209
Garnet red*	816	20	0512
⊟ Topaz yellow	725	306	0108
⧌ White	White	2	White
⦁ Light peach	754	6	0305
Medium peach*	352	9	0303
■ Medium brown	433	371	2008
‖ Pale grey	415	398	1803
Z Tan brown	436	363	2011
⊡ Medium mahogany brown	301	349	2306

Note: outline medium topaz brown with dark golden brown; black with steel grey*; off white with golden wheat*; bright orange with garnet red*, and light peach with medium peach* (starred colours are used for bks only), and make the eyes with french knots in medium brown.*

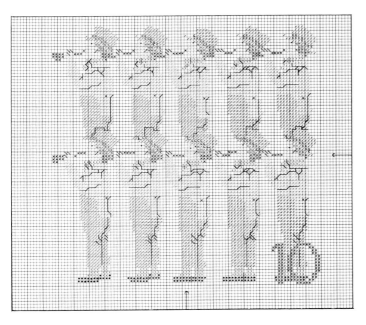

TENTH DAY OF CHRISTMAS ◄		DMC	ANCHOR	MADEIRA
☒	Gold thread	—	—	—
⊡	Light peach	754	6	0305
	Medium peach*	352	9	0303
◉	Medium beige grey	644	830	1907
	Very dark beige grey*	640	903	1905
▯	White	White	2	White
	Light steel grey*	318	399	1802
⧄	Light blue	813	160	1013
	Dark blue*	825	162	1011
⊡	Bright Christmas red	666	46	0210
	Dark garnet red*	814	44	0514
Ⓒ	Topaz yellow	725	306	0108
⦀	Tan brown	436	363	2011
⊞	Medium brown	433	371	2008

Note: outline light peach with medium peach; medium beige grey with very dark beige grey*; white with light steel grey*; light blue with dark blue*, and bright Christmas red with dark garnet red*, and make french knots with medium brown.*

ELEVENTH DAY OF CHRISTMAS ►		DMC	ANCHOR	MADEIRA
☒	Gold thread	—	—	—
⊡	Light peach	754	6	0305
	Medium peach*	352	9	0303
Ⓒ	Melon orange	3340	329	0214
	Medium salmon red*	3328	11	0408
⊡	Light violet	554	96	0711
	Dark violet*	552	100	0713
⊟	Light old gold	676	891	2208
	Dark old gold*	680	901	2210
▽	Silver thread	—	—	—
⧄	Aqua	959	186	1113
	Medium aqua*	943	188	1203
▯	White	White	2	White
	Light steel grey*	318	399	1802
⦀	Hazelnut brown	869	944	2105

Note: outline light peach with medium peach; melon orange with medium salmon red*; light violet with dark violet*; light old gold with dark old gold*; aqua with medium aqua*, and white with light steel grey*, and the eyes with french knots in hazelnut brown (starred colours are used for bks only).*

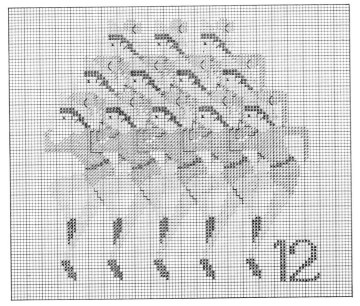

TWELFTH DAY OF CHRISTMAS ◄		DMC	ANCHOR	MADEIRA
☒	Gold thread	—	—	—
⊡	Light peach	754	6	0305
	Medium peach*	352	9	0303
⦀	Light brown	434	309	2009
Ⓞ	Medium topaz brown	782	307	2212
▯	White	White	2	White
	Light steel grey*	318	399	1802
⧄	Bright orange	608	333	0206
	Medium Christmas red*	304	47	0509
⊡	Kelly green	702	226	1306
	Christmas green*	699	923	1303

Note: outline light peach with medium peach; white with light steel grey*; bright orange with medium Christmas red*, and Kelly green with Christmas green* (starred colours are used for bks only).*

Christmas Cards

Personalized greetings cards containing a small embroidery are a pleasure to make or receive. Christmas cards first became popular in the late Victorian era. Early cards were decorated with flowers, then came the more traditional Christmas themes, such as holly, robins and snow scenes, followed by nativities and angels.

CHRISTMAS CARDS

YOU WILL NEED

For each card, the large cards measuring
16cm × 11cm (6¼in × 4¼in), and the small
cards 9cm × 12cm (3¼in × 4½in):

*Stranded embroidery cotton in the colours given in
the appropriate panel
No 26 tapestry needle
Double-sided adhesive tape
Appropriate card, as listed below (for suppliers, see
page 48)*

●

For the *Bethlehem* card:

9cm × 12cm (3¼in × 4½in) of sky blue,
22-count Hardanger
Small Christmas red card with a rectangular
cut-out

For the *Santa* card:

9cm × 12cm (3¼in × 4½in) of silver fleck,
20-count Bellana fabric
Small Christmas red card with a rectangular
cut-out

For the *Robins* card:

16cm × 11cm (6¼in × 4¼in) of silver fleck,
20-count Bellana fabric
Large Christmas red card with an oval cut-out

For the *Nöel* card:

16cm × 11cm (6¼in × 4¼in) of white, 18-count
Aida fabric
Large holly green card with a rectangular cut-out

For the *Xmas* card:

16cm × 11cm (6¼in × 4¼in) of silver fleck,
20-count Bellana fabric
Large holly green card with a circular cut-out

For the *Shepherd* card:

16cm × 11cm (6¼in × 4¼in) of white, 20-count
Bellana fabric
Large holly green card with an oval cut-out

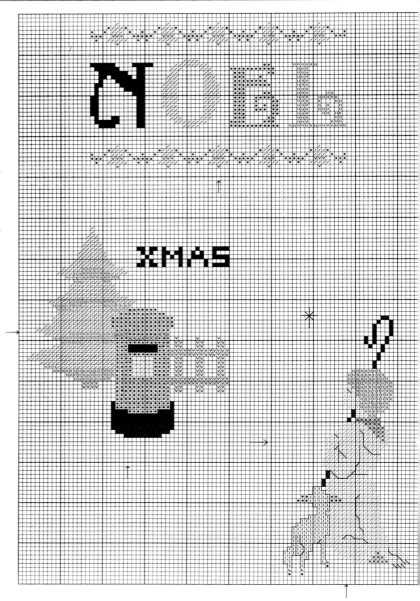

THE EMBROIDERY

Each card is made in the same way. To economize
on fabric, you could make the *Santa*, *Robins*, and
Xmas cards on a single piece of fabric, providing
you leave sufficient space around each design.

Prepare the fabric, marking the centre (of each
design, if you are stitching several on a single
piece) with horizontal and vertical lines of basting
stitches (see page 4). Set the fabric in a hoop, and
complete the cross stitch embroidery, using one
strand of embroidery cotton in the needle throughout. When you have completed the embroidery,
gently press the finished piece from the wrong side,
leaving the basting stitches in postition at this stage.

NÖEL ◄		DMC	ANCHOR	MADEIRA
⊙	Dark Kelly green	701	227	1305
╱	Topaz yellow	725	306	0108
⋁	Medium topaz yellow	782	307	2212
■	Bright Christmas red	666	46	0210
⫴	Dark violet	552	100	0713

XMAS ◄		DMC	ANCHOR	MADEIRA
■	Black	310	403	Black
╱	Kelly green	702	226	0306
⫴	Christmas green	699	923	1303
⋁	Medium brown	433	371	2008
⊠	Dark Christmas red	498	47	0511
⊙	Light red	350	11	0213
⦂	White	White	2	White

SHEPHERD ◄		DMC	ANCHOR	MADEIRA
■	Medium brown	433	371	2008
⫴	Very light brown	435	365	2010
•	Light peach	754	6	0305
	Medium peach*	352	9	0303
⊠	Dark antique mauve	315	896	0810
⦂	Antique mauve	316	894	0809
⊡	White	White	2	White
⊙	Black	310	403	Black
L	Light steel grey	318	399	1802
	Silver thread*	—	—	—

Note: bks around light peach with medium peach; white with light steel grey, and star with silver thread* (starred colours used for bks only).*

BETHLEHEM ►		DMC	ANCHOR	MADEIRA
⊙	Silver thread	—	—	—
■	Black	310	403	Black
•	White	White	2	White
╱	Light peach	754	6	0305
⫴	Dark aqua	958	187	1114
L	Light steel grey	318	399	1802
⋁	Light loden green	3364	843	1512
⊠	Dark loden green	3362	846	1514

SANTA ►		DMC	ANCHOR	MADEIRA
■	Bright Christmas red	666	46	0210
⦂	Light peach	754	6	0305
⦂	White	White	2	White
	Light steel grey*	318	399	1802
⫴	Kelly green	702	226	0306
⊙	Black	310	403	Black
⋁	Medium peach	352	9	0303

Note: bks string in black; around white with light steel grey (used for bks only), and around light peach with medium peach.*

ROBINS ►		DMC	ANCHOR	MADEIRA
⦂	Pale grey	415	398	1803
■	Black	310	403	Black
⊙	Dark forest brown	938	381	2005
╱	Medium brown	433	371	2008
•	Medium yellow	744	301	0112
⊡	Very light mahogany brown	402	347	2307
⫴	Light red	350	11	0213

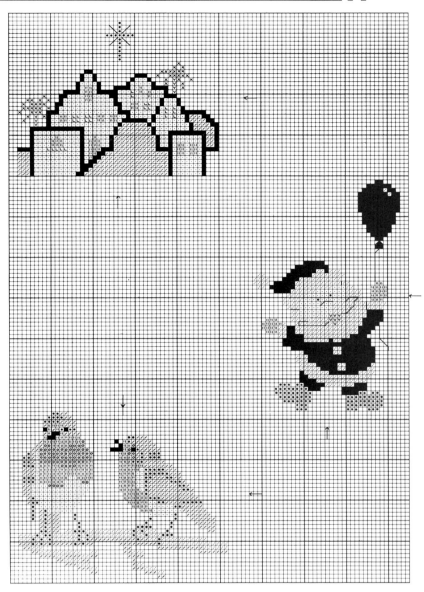

MAKING UP THE CARDS

Trim the embroidery to measure slightly larger all around than the card window, then centre it behind the window, using the basting stitches as guidelines. Make light pencil marks on the back of the embroidery and the back of the window, to act as registration marks. Remove the basting stitches, then replace the card in the window. Use double-sided tape to secure the card in position, then press the backing down firmly.

Christmas Stocking

This lovely embroidered stocking is just the right size to hold small sweets and toys, or a small teddy. It is a present which will delight any child at Christmas.

CHRISTMAS STOCKING

YOU WILL NEED

For the Christmas stocking, measuring approximately 31cm × 28cm (12½in × 11¼in):

Two 38cm × 30.5cm (15in × 12in) pieces of holly green, 14-count Aida fabric
1.5m (1⅔yds) of red bias binding, 12mm (½in) wide
Stranded embroidery cotton in the colours given in the panel
No24 tapestry needle
Red sewing thread

•

THE EMBROIDERY

Take one of the two pieces of Aida fabric; prepare it for embroidery and set it in a hoop or frame (see page 4). Embroider the design; work the cross stitch first, using two strands of embroidery cotton in the needle, and then the backstitch, using one strand.

Gently press the finished embroidery on the wrong side, using a steam iron.

MAKING THE STOCKING

Trace the stocking template on good quality tracing paper, marking the position of the arrows. Centre this over the embroidery; mark and then cut out the shape. Reversing the tracing paper pattern, cut a mirror-image shape from the remaining piece of Aida.

Place the two pieces with wrong sides together and baste around the edge. Machine stitch, taking a 12mm (½in) seam allowance and leaving the top open. Trim the edge to within 6m (¼in) of the stitching line and remove basting stitches.

Pin and baste the red bias binding all around the stitched edge and around the open top edge of the stocking. Stitching through all layers, stitch the binding in position. If you intend to hang the stocking, make a small hanging loop from a short length of the binding and stitch this to the top of the stocking, at the back seam.

◀ Each square measures 2½cm (1in)

STOCKING ▶		DMC	ANCHOR	MADEIRA
☑	Bright Christmas red	666	46	0210
C	Medium garnet red	815	43	0513
•	White	White	2	White
☒	Topaz yellow	725	306	0108
●	Black	310	403	Black
‖	Medium steel grey	317	400	1714
•	Light peach	754	6	0305
∧	Medium peach	352	9	0303
H	Medium Delft blue	799	130	0910
V	Royal blue	797	132	0912
I	Golden wheat	3046	887	2206
O	Dark golden wheat	3045	888	2103
≡	Medium violet	553	98	0712
L	Light Chartreuse green	704	256	1308
Z	Very light golden yellow	3078	292	0102

Note: bks white with medium steel grey; light peach with medium peach and golden wheat with dark golden wheat.

Cake Band and Glass Coasters

Complement your cake with this pretty cake band, which you can keep and re-use for years to come. A set of glass coasters with snowflake motifs provides the perfect finishing touch to your Christmas table.

CAKE BAND AND GLASS COASTERS

SNOWFLAKES ▶	DMC	ANCHOR	MADEIRA
White	White	2	White

YOU WILL NEED

For the cake band, measuring 85cm × 10cm
(33½in × 4in):

*87.5cm (34½in) of green Aida band, 10cm (4in)
deep, with silver edging
Silver thread
No 24 tapestry needle
Sewing thread to match the Aida*

For a set of six coasters, each 7cm (2¾in) in
diameter:

*27cm × 18cm (10¾in × 7in) of navy, 18-count
Aida fabric
27cm × 18cm (10¾in × 7in) of ultra-soft,
medium-weight, iron-on interfacing
Stranded embroidery cotton as given in
the appropriate panel
No 26 tapestry needle
Six glass coasters (for suppliers, see page 48)*

•

CAKE BAND

Use silver metallic thread and centre the design
along the Aida band, remembering to leave 12mm
(½in) clear at each end for the seam allowances.
Embroider the cross stitch design; there are 14
pattern repeats.

When you have finished the embroidery, turn
under a double 6mm (¼in) hem at each short end.
Attach the band to the cake either with pins or with
small blobs of icing.

GLASS COASTERS

Divide the Aida fabric with lines of basting stitches
into six equal sections. Set the fabric in a hoop or
frame and complete the cross stitch embroidery,
using two strands of embroidery cotton in the
needle throughout, and ensuring that each design
is centred within a section, When you have
finished, remove basting stitches, and press.

Iron the interfacing to the wrong side of your
fabric. This will prevent fraying, and will also
enable you to see the pencil lines made when you
draw around the paper templates provided with the
coasters. You may, however, find it easier to use a
pair of compasses to draw a 6cm (2¼in) circle on
the interfacing around each design (make sure that
they are centred within their circles).

For each coaster, cut a fabric circle and place it
in the recess on the base of a coaster. Put a paper
template on the reverse side of the embroidery, then
peel the backing from the protective base and
carefully place it over the back of the coaster,
ensuring that the embroidery and template remain
in position.

CAKE BAND ▶
Silver thread

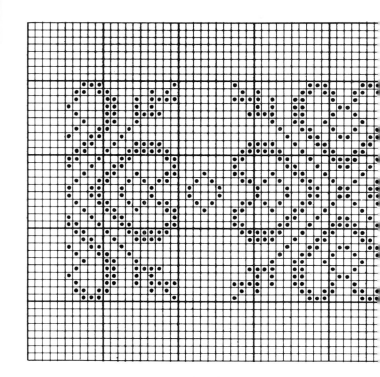

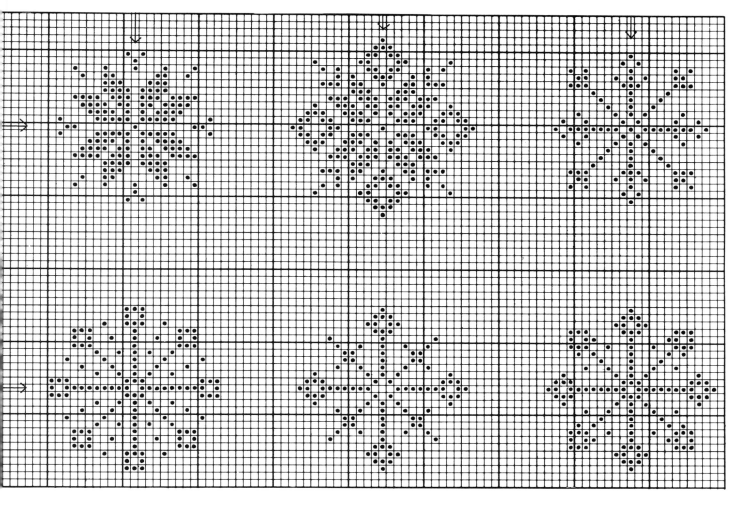

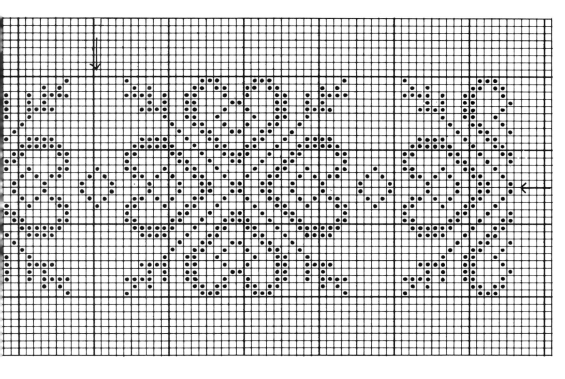

Advent Calendar

During the first weeks of December, everyone is busy preparing for the holiday, and children use an advent calendar to count the days until Christmas. This colourful bellpull hides pockets holding a small present for each day. Children will love discovering the tiny gifts in their numbered pockets, one for each day up to Christmas Eve.

ADVENT CALENDAR

YOU WILL NEED

For the advent calendar, measuring 12.5cm × 60cm (5in × 24in):

15cm × 1.27m (6in × 50in) strip of silver fleck, 20-count Bellana this includes a 12mm (½in) seam allowance all around
Stranded embroidery cotton in the colour given in the panel
A mixture of sequins
Seed pearls
White sewing cotton
No 26 tapestry needle
Beading needle
Brass bell-pull ends, 14cm (5½in) wide

•

MAKING THE CALENDAR

Using a sewing machine, zigzag around the raw edges of the fabric to prevent it from fraying. You may find that it is easier to work the embroidery without mounting the fabric in a hoop or frame. Starting 3.5cm (1½in) down from the top edge, embroider the numbers, using three strands of embroidery cotton in the needle and stitching over two threads of the Bellana (making 10 stitches per 2.5cm (1in). Decorate the numbers with sequins and seed pearls, positioning these at random, as seen in the photograph.

Turn in the 12mm (½in) seam allowance down the long sides and machine stitch, a scant 6mm (¼in) in from the folded edge. Taking a 6mm (¼in) seam allowance, and with wrong sides together, join the two short edges of the fabric. Stitching through both layers of fabric, mark out the stitching lines with basting stitches, as shown on the chart. Machine stitch along all the basting lines, forming the side pockets. Slide the top and bottom bell-pull ends through the slots in the fabric.

Small gifts can now be wrapped in tissue paper and placed inside the pockets.

ADVENT CALENDAR ▶	DMC	ANCHOR	MADEIRA
☑ Bright Christmas red	666	46	0210
— Stitching line for pockets			

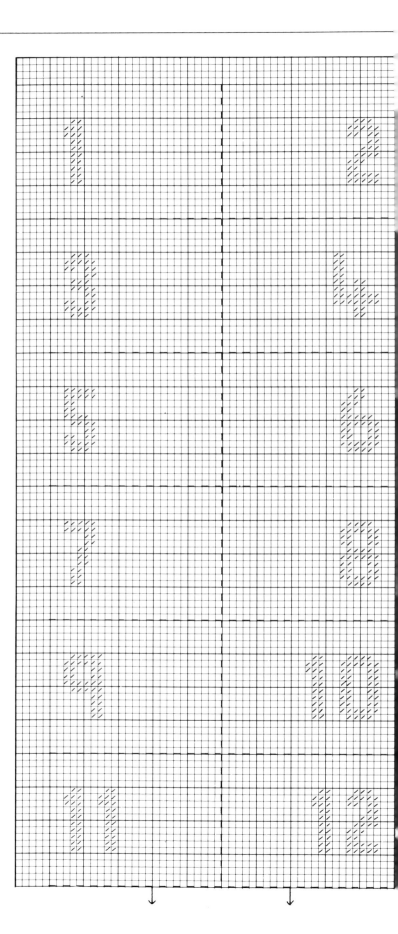

ACKNOWLEDGEMENTS

The Author would like to thank the following people for their help with this book:

For the embroidery work: Odette Harrison, Linda Potter, Libby Shaw, Lesley Buckerfield, Stella Baddeley and Dawn-Marie Parmley.

For making up the projects: Louise Wells.

For supplying items and fabrics for use in this book: DMC Creative World Ltd (*for the fabrics and cards*)

Framecraft Miniatures Ltd ('*Christmas shapes' tree decorations, glass coasters, glass bowls, table linen – from their Sal-em range, gift tags, placecards and serviette holders*).

Both suppliers request that a stamped self-addressed envelope be enclosed with all enquiries.

SUPPLIERS

The following mail order company has supplied some of the basic items needed for making up the projects in this book:

Framecraft Miniatures Limited
372/376 Summer Lane
Hockley
Birmingham, B19 3QA
England
Telephone (021) 359 4442

Addresses for Framecraft stockists worldwide
Ireland Needlecraft Pty Ltd
2-4 Keppel Drive
Hallam, Victoria 3803
Australia

Danish Art Needlework
PO Box 442, Lethbridge
Alberta T1J 3Z1
Canada

Sanyei Imports
PO Box 5, Hashima Shi
Gifu 501-62
Japan

The Embroidery Shop
286 Queen Street
Masterton
New Zealand

Anne Brinkley Designs Inc.
246 Walnut Street
Newton
Mass. 02160
USA

S A Threads and Cottons Ltd.
43 Somerset Road
Cape Town
South Africa

For information on your nearest stockist of embroidery cotton, contact the following:

DMC

UK
DMC Creative World Limited
62 Pullman Road
Wigston
Leicester, LE8 2DY
Telephone: 0533 811040

USA
The DMC Corporation
Port Kearney Bld.
10 South Kearney
N.J. 07032-0650
Telephone: 201 589 0606

AUSTRALIA
DMC Needlecraft Pty
P.O. Box 317
Earlswood 2206
NSW 2204
Telephone: 02599 3088

COATS AND ANCHOR

UK
Kilncraigs Mill
Alloa
Clackmannanshire
Scotland, FK10 1EG
Telephone: 0259 723431

USA
Coats & Clark
P.O. Box 27067
Dept CO1
Greenville
SC 29616
Telephone: 803 234 0103

AUSTRALIA
Coats Patons Crafts
Thistle Street
Launceston
Tasmania 7250
Telephone: 00344 4222

MADEIRA

UK
Madeira Threads (UK) Limited
Thirsk Industrial Park
York Road, Thirsk
N. Yorkshire, YO7 3BX
Telephone: 0845 524880

USA
Madeira Marketing Limited
600 East 9th Street
Michigan City
IN 46360
Telephone: 219 873 1000

AUSTRALIA
Penguin Threads Pty Limited
25-27 Izett Street
Prahran
Victoria 3181
Telephone: 03529 4400